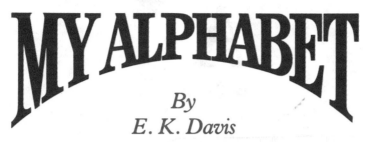

MY ALPHABET

By
E. K. Davis

Illustrated

A GOLDEN BOOK • NEW YORK
Western Publishing Company, Inc., Racine, Wisconsin 53404

Text copyright © 1981 by Western Publishing Company, Inc. Illustrations copyright © 1981 by Pat Stewart. All rights reserved. Printed in the U.S.A. No part of this book may be reproduced or copied in any form without written permission from the publisher. GOLDEN®, GOLDEN & DESIGN®, A FIRST LITTLE GOLDEN BOOK®, FIRST LITTLE GOLDEN BOOKS®, LITTLE GOLDEN BOOKS®, and A GOLDEN BOOK® are trademarks of Western Publishing Company, Inc. Library of Congress Catalog Card Number: 80-85086 ISBN 0-307-10104-5/ISBN 0-307-68104-1 (lib. bdg.)

U V W X Y Z

A is for apple,
Red and bright.

B is for bed,
Where I sleep at night.

CONCORDIA UNIVERSITY LIBRARY
PORTLAND, OR 97211

C is for carrot,
Crunchy and yummy.

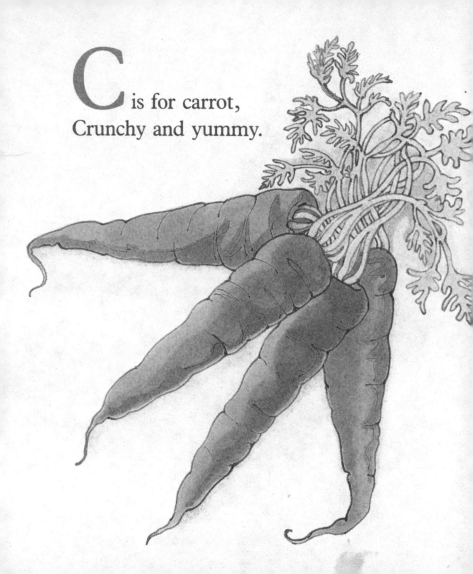

D is for dog.
He lies on his tummy.

E

is for elephant.
She likes a shower.

F is for flag.
It flies from a tower.

G is for grapes.
They grow in a bunch.

H is for hamster.
She's eating her lunch.

I is for ice cream,
Cold and sweet.

J is for jelly.
What a nice treat!

K is for kitten,
Playing with yarn.

L is for lamb.
He lives in the barn.

M is for mirror.
I see my face!

N is for nest,
In a high place.

O is for owl,
Flying at night.

P is for pear.
Have a big bite!

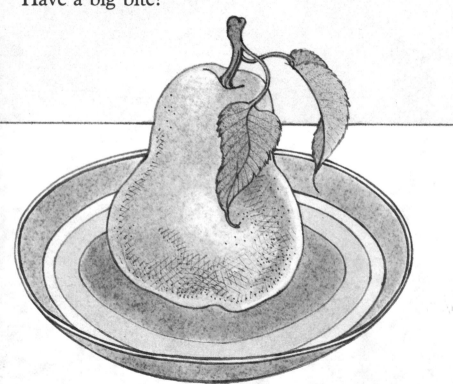

Q is for quilt,
All cozy and warm.

R is for rainbow,
After a storm.

S is for sun.
It shines in the sky.

T is for telephone.
Say "Hello!" and
"Good-by!"

U is for umbrella.
The rain won't come through.

I Love You

V is for valentine.
It says "I love you."

W is for watch.
Listen, it ticks!

X is for xylophone.
Make music with sticks.

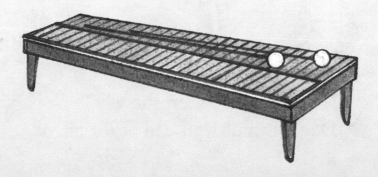

C.Lit PE 1155 .D38 1981
Davis, E. K. 1937-
My alphabet

Y is for yo-yo.
It goes down, then
comes back.

Z is for zebra
With stripes
white and black.

Now you have seen the whole alphabet.
Do you think you can say it all yet?